Amazing Cars

Amazing Cars

WRITTEN BY
TREVOR LORD

PHOTOGRAPHED BY
DAVE KING

ALFRED A. KNOPF • NEW YORK

Conceived and produced by
Dorling Kindersley Limited

Project editor Louise Pritchard
Art editor Mark Regardsoe
Senior art editor Julia Harris
Senior editor Helen Parker
Production Shelagh Gibson

Illustrations by Bruce Hogarth and Julie Anderson
Cars supplied by National Motor Museum at Beaulieu; John Lewis (pp 14-15);
Keith Atkinson (pp 16-17); International Automotive Design (pp 24-25)
Special thanks to Carl Gombrich for research; Mike Dunning for photography (pp 24-25);
Andy Saunders for his "Amazing minis" (p 17)

Chitty Chitty Bang Bang by permission of Warfield Productions Inc.;
James Bond Aston Martin DB5 by permission of Eon Productions Ltd

This is a Borzoi Book published by Alfred A. Knopf, Inc.

Library of Congress Cataloging in Publication Data
Lord, Trevor.
Amazing cars / written by Trevor Lord.
p. cm. – (Eyewitness juniors)
Includes index.
Summary: Introduces the history, uses, and different styles of cars. Also
discusses famous cars and cars of the future.
1. Automobiles – Juvenile literature. [1. Automobiles.]
I. Title. II. Series.
TL147.L59 1992 629.2–dc20 91-53138
ISBN 0-679-82766-8
ISBN 0-679-92766-2 (lib. bdg.)

Color reproduction by Colourscan, Singapore
Printed in Italy by A. Mondadori Editore, Verona

Contents

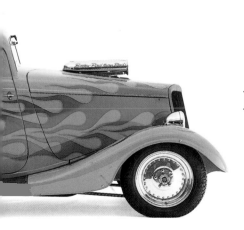

What is a car?

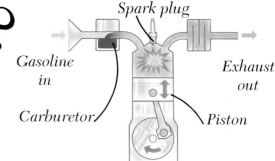

Spark plug

Gasoline in

Carburetor

Exhaust out

Piston

In the last 100 years, few things have changed our lives and the look of our surroundings more than the car. It is a truly amazing invention.

How does it work?

Most cars are powered by a gasoline engine. Gasoline is mixed with air in the carburetor. A spark from a spark plug makes this mixture explode. This pushes a piston down, which turns the car's wheels.

Sun roof rolled back

On wheels

A car would be useless without wheels. It is moved and steered by the wheels and stopped by the brakes, which are connected to the wheels. The tires are filled with air to make the ride comfortable.

Trunk for luggage

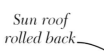

H359 FJ

Farm vehicle

The Citroën 2CV was designed in the 1930s for use in rural areas. The designers were asked to make a car which would carry two people and 100 pounds of produce or a small barrel, and drive over a field carrying a box of eggs without breaking any.

Slow moving

There are millions of cars in the world today, and roads get overcrowded. The average speed of traffic in some cities is the same now as it was before we had cars!

Altered to fit

Cars can be altered to suit disabled people. For example, the brakes can be controlled by hand instead of by foot.

How many are there?

Cars are useful, but they cause problems. The people on the British island of Sark do not have cars – only bicycles and horse-drawn carts.

Hood

Is this a car?

A car is a motorized vehicle that carries passengers on the road. Most cars are easy to recognize, but some don't look like cars at all.

Happy families

A car can be one of the family. It goes shopping and may go on vacation. Some people even give their cars a name!

A 2CV is just over 12 feet long. Its top speed is 70 miles per hour (mph).

Birth of the car

The first cars did not look like cars at all. Many of the ideas were copied from other kinds of transportation.

Horseless carriages

Some early cars were simply horse-drawn carriages fitted with an engine. These cars were difficult to steer without the help of the horses.

Making claims

In 1895, the Pennington Company told people that its car could carry nine people, drive at 40 mph, and had puncture-proof tires. This of course was not true!

Uphill struggle

In early cars, the gas tank was placed up high so that the gas could flow down to the engine. But if the car was driven up a very steep hill, the gas would flow away from the engine. The solution was to drive up backward!

Right or wrong

Small boats are steered using a tiller. Some of the first cars were also steered using a tiller. To turn the car to the right, the tiller was moved to the left. To turn the car to the left, the tiller was moved to the right – confusing!

Tiller

This Peugeot is 8½ feet long

Tiring journey

The first cars shared the roads with many horses. Nails from the horses' shoes often caused flat tires. Drivers expected a flat on every journey.

Safety in numbers

Until 1896, the British speed limit for cars in towns was 2 mph – about as fast as you walk! And to be safe, each car had to carry two people, with a third person walking in front to warn that it was coming.

Hot seat

Passengers in a quadricycle had no protection in an accident, and the engine was under the driver's seat. No wonder this car was unpopular!

"Handlebars"

Tubular frame

Basket

Part bicycle

Peugeot made bicycles before it made cars. It used its bicycle ideas on this 1896 car.

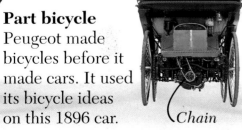

Chain

Spoked wheel

On the road

Sports cars are the fastest cars on the road, and they are built to be fun to drive. No one worries about the comfort of the passenger – if there is one!

Gliding along

The Mercedes Gullwing is very low. To make it easier to get in and out, the doors open upward, making the car look like a flying gull.

To begin with

One of the first sports cars was the Vauxhall Prince Henry, with a top speed of 75 mph. This is slow for today, but it was fast for 1915, when the car was made.

Happy birthday

In 1987, the Italian Ferrari company was 40 years old. To celebrate, they built a new, very special and very fast supercar called the F40. Only a few were made.

Beetle in disguise

This Porsche 911 was designed by the grandson of Ferdinand Porsche, the designer of the Volkswagen Beetle. Parts of these cars look the same, but the Porsche goes much faster than the Beetle.

This Porsche is about 14 feet long from nose to tail

Looks good

One of the top sports cars in the 1950s was the Corvette. It had stunning good looks and could accelerate even faster than a Jaguar.

Fast and fashionable

In the 1960s the most fashionable car was the Jaguar E-Type. It was fast too, with a top speed of 150 mph.

Do It Yourself

Lotus built only about 3,000 of their Lotus 7 sports cars, and most of them were sold as kits. The customer bought the parts and, luckily, a set of instructions.

That's fast!

The top speed of the Lamborghini Diablo is over 200 mph. It is claimed to be the fastest road car in the world. The huge engine can rocket the car from a standstill to 60 mph in less than 4 seconds!

"Spoiler" to push the car down onto the road for better grip

Working cars

Many cars are specially built to go to work every day and do a job. Others are everyday cars modified, or changed, to do special jobs.

Called up
Cars were first used as ambulances during the First World War (1914-1918). They were modified to carry the wounded to the hospital. Many nurses learned to drive as part of their training.

Just like a frog
An amphibian is an animal that lives on land and in water, such as a frog. We call cars that can travel on land and in water "amphibious." Amphibious cars can be useful for getting close to wildlife.

Making tracks
The first car to cross the Sahara Desert in Africa had tracks at the rear instead of wheels. The tracks gave a better grip and prevented the car from sinking into the soft sand.

Symbol to show taxi takes a wheel-chair

"For hire" light

London taxi
This car is specially designed and built to be a taxi. It has room for luggage in the front, next to the driver, and extra seats that flip down so the taxi can carry five people.

H166 WYW

Fast worker

Police often drive at high speeds. Their cars have flashing lights so we can see them coming – and a loud siren so we can hear them too!

Moving pictures

At sports events, television companies often put a camera on a car so the camera person can keep up with the action.

To the rescue

Some organizations help motorists whose cars have broken down. A mechanic comes in a tow truck with some of the tools and spare parts you would find in a garage.

This London taxi is 17³/₄ feet long from bumper to bumper

Flip-down seat

E8005

Crazy cars

Cars are not always just the way their owners want them. So they are customized – chopped up, added to, given new parts, and painted bright colors – until they look completely different.

Swanning along
This swan car was made in 1912. Its beak opens and shuts, its nostrils are exhaust pipes, and its eyes are electric lights.

War hero
"Jeepneys" were first built in the Philippines from American jeeps left behind after the Second World War. Today they are made using parts from more modern cars.

The roof has been lowered 4 inches

Just my imagination...
You can do almost anything you like to a car. With time and imagination, you can turn an ordinary car into a work of art.

The wheel wells have been enlarged to make room for these new wide wheels

Ahoy there!
This car used to be a speedboat. Now, with three wheels, it is only for cruising the roads.

Amazing minis
These two Minis are even more mini than usual! They are ideal for squeezing in and out of small spaces, making parking much less of a problem.

Scoop for taking in air to cool the engine

Orange squash
Under the skin, this orange car is just a Mini. There is very little room inside, so the passengers are often squashed.

One in a thousand
In 1934 this Ford Sedan was like all the others. Today, it is lower, has a 7.5-liter Chevrolet engine, and can hit a top speed of 140 mph.

This customized Ford is now over 16 feet long

Traveling in style

Some cars are built for speed; some are made to run cheaply. Other cars are designed to provide luxury, no matter what the cost.

Cadillac comfort

This 1957 Cadillac is still thought to be luxurious today. Among its features are separate heating in the front and back, and seats which move electrically and store favorite positions in a memory.

Power guzzler

A "super-luxury" eight-seater Mercedes-Benz was introduced in the 1960s. Its many power-assisted features required one sixth of the engine's power.

Quality car

Duesenberg cars were made in the U.S. to rival the British Rolls-Royce. They claimed to be "the world's finest automobiles." Only about 36 Duesenberg SJs were built.

This 1935 Duesenberg SJ is about 16 feet long

Don't spill it

The Rolls-Royce is famous for its smooth, quiet ride. In the 1930s, pupils at the Rolls-Royce school for chauffeurs had to drive this Phantom II with a glass of water balanced on the radiator – without spilling it!

Top class

The inside of this 1906 Renault was copied from a first-class railway carriage. The owner had wanted a tall car in which he would be able to wear his top hat.

Golf-club locker

Anyone for golf?

This 1935 Auburn was popular with Hollywood film stars. It was one of the first cars to have a radio. There was no room for luggage, but there was a special locker for golf clubs instead.

Fit for a king

Leopold II was king of Belgium from 1865 to 1909. He was a large man so he had a car specially made, with a wide seat shaped like his favorite armchair. His design became popular and was known as "Roi des Belges" style.

Duesenberg mascot known as a Duesenbird

Outside exhaust pipes

On the track

 Ever since cars first appeared, people have wanted to see who could drive the fastest. Racing in cars is now a popular sport. It is exciting, but it can also be dangerous.

In the right gear

Racing drivers today wear a crash helmet and a special suit to protect them in an accident. The first racing drivers just wore a cap – back to front so it wouldn't blow off!

Racing 'round the clock

One of the world's most famous car races is the Le Mans 24 Hours, in France. Every year, teams of drivers race their cars all through the day and night.

Smooth tires used in dry weather

What a drag

Dragsters are the most powerful of all racing cars and can reach a speed of more than 250 mph in only 5 seconds. A drag race takes place between two cars along a straight-line course which is only a quarter-mile long.

It's the pits

If a racing car needs new tires during a race, the driver goes into the pit, where the mechanics can change all four wheels in less than 10 seconds. Sometimes they have to refuel the car or change worn-out parts.

Hugging the road

The fan on the back of this racing car pulls the air out from under the car. This draws the car closer to the race track and helps it go around the corners faster.

Leading the way

When motor racing began, ordinary cars were raced along ordinary roads. Drivers were often led through the smaller towns by a cyclist to keep them from breaking the speed limit. A mechanic traveled in each car in case of a breakdown.

Racing on wings

The "wings" on a Formula One racing car work just like an airplane's wings – but upside down. They hold the car down instead of lifting it up.

This Formula One car is over 14 feet long and 7 feet wide

—"Wing"

Famous cars

Cars, like people, can become famous for many reasons. How many of these famous cars do you recognize?

Tasty Rolls

For some people, even a Rolls-Royce is not good enough. Pop star John Lennon made his Rolls-Royce easy to recognize with a special paint job.

Popemobile

The popemobile is a converted Range Rover used by Pope John Paul II. It is designed to give the crowd a good view of the pope as he travels around. The car has special puncture-proof tires, and there are handles and a step at the back for the pope's bodyguards.

Speeding? Me?

When the first motorways were opened in Britain, there was no speed limit. Early one morning, in 1964, an AC Cobra racing car was tested at over 180 mph. Not surprisingly, a motorway speed limit of 70 mph was introduced in Britain soon after!

Chitty Chitty Bang Bang is just over 22 feet long, including the basket

Wing for flying

Over the moon

In 1971 the Apollo 15 spacecraft took the first car to the moon. This electric vehicle cost about $60 million to build and took 10 years to design.

No-rust guarantee

DeLorean cars were made famous by the *Back to the Future* films, in which the car was a time machine. DeLoreans are special in real life too. They are not painted, but they never rust because they are made of stainless steel.

Full of tricks

The film version of James Bond's Aston Martin DB5 had lots of special gadgets. It could produce an oil slick to slow down chasing cars, and it had a bulletproof shield at the back and an ejector seat to remove unwanted passengers!

Goes with a bang

The *Chitty Chitty Bang Bang* film car was based on real cars that raced in Britain in the 1920s. They got their name because their noisy engine went chitty-chitty-bang-bang!

Oar lock for holding an oar when rowing

In the film, Chitty Chitty Bang Bang could travel on the road, in the air, and on water

Into the future

Exciting new cars are being developed all the time. Most will not be built to go faster than cars can today, but will be designed to make driving safer and easier.

A bright idea

Sunraycer runs on solar energy. It has special panels that change sunlight into electrical energy. Unfortunately, solar-powered cars work well only in countries that have a lot of sunshine!

Keep your distance

In the future, drivers may be forced to drive safely because of sensors placed in the car and under the road. The sensors will detect when a car is too close to the one in front and stop it from getting any closer.

Quieter towns

Battery-powered cars cause less pollution than gas-powered cars. They are being developed to travel long distances without having to have their batteries recharged.

No more maps

One day, drivers will not need maps. They will tell a computer in the car where they want to go, and the computer will work out the best route. It will also find out how to avoid traffic jams and bad weather.

Parking made easy

The problem of parking could soon disappear. Volkswagen has built a car that can park itself. The driver just stands by and watches!

Venus is about 13 feet long

Home, James

Over 90% of road accidents are the fault of the driver. One day computers may do the driving. A computer would not drive too fast, get tired, or ignore a red light. And it would not drink too much alcohol either.

A view of the future

Venus is an experimental car – the only one of its kind to be built. It has two cameras to help the driver see the road in bad conditions. The cameras film in front and behind and show the views on a screen in the car.

Wheel inside "tire-hugging pod" to stop road spray

Making a car

Cars are now made in many parts of the world. Over the years, the ways in which cars are made have changed as much as the cars themselves.

Any color you like

Henry Ford's Model T was the first car to be made on a moving production line. Ford said that people could have a Model T in any color – as long as it was black!

Cars from rock

Today, car factories are as big as towns. Until recently at Ford's factory in Dagenham, England, iron ore (from which steel is made) arrived by ship at one end of the factory and cars came out the other.

BE 278

This 1914 Model T is 12 feet long and 5 feet wide

Five years old
It can take five years for a new car to appear in the showroom. A design is drawn first, often on a computer, so that changes can be easily made.

Model car
A clay model is built to test the shape and see, for example, how well the car will cut through the air. Changes are then made to the design, if necessary.

Road test
Full-size working models are tested to see that the car runs well and is safe, and to see what would happen in a crash. Then real production begins.

Built by robot
Today, robots are often used to make the body of cars. Robots can put on wheels and paint the bodies, but they do not drive the cars – yet!

Body work
When cars first became popular, makers of horse-drawn carriages began making car bodies instead.

What a difference
Aston Martin builds 200 cars a year, and Toyota makes 5 million. So while Aston Martin is making one car, Toyota is making 25,000!

Record breakers

Since the beginning of motoring, some cars have stood out from all the others and now have a place in history. They are the record breakers.

Tail fin kept the car straight

Airplane on wheels
Donald Campbell drove *Bluebird* for a new land speed record (403.10 mph) in 1964. It is easy to imagine this car with wings. Who knows? Perhaps it would have flown.

We love the Beetles
The Volkswagen Beetle was first made in 1938. It is no longer sold in the U.S., but over 20 million have sold worldwide, making it the most popular car of all time.

The lengths people go to
One of the largest cars ever built was made in California. It has 26 wheels and is nearly 100 feet long. It has a swimming pool and a helicopter landing pad. When it has to turn a corner it just bends in the middle.

A long way to go
A Honda car, *Genius E*, broke the record for the lowest rate of gas consumption – 6,409 miles per gallon. If all cars could do this, most drivers would only have to buy gasoline once every five years!

Fastest on land

In 1983 Richard Noble broke the land speed record. His jet-engined car *Thrust 2* sped across 1 mile of Black Rock Desert in California – twice – at an average speed of just over 633 mph.

On your bike

The first official land speed record was set in 1898 at 39 mph. This was slower than the cycling record at the time!

Give me a lift

At 52 inches long, the Peel is one of the smallest cars ever made. It has no reverse gear. The driver just gets out, grabs the handle at the back, and lifts the car around.

Driver's cockpit

Bluebird *is over 30 feet long*